Chris -

this book reminds
me of you. Thanks
for being the special
person you are.

w/ love
Liz

Feb. '96

COME WALK AMONG THE STARS

Come Walk Among the Stars

Words by
WINSTON O. ABBOTT
Drawings by
BETTE EATON BOSSEN

Published by
INSPIRATION HOUSE
South Windsor, Connecticut

FIFTEENTH PRINTING 1988

ISBN 0-918114-00-4

This book is a companion volume to

SING WITH THE WIND

HAVE YOU HEARD THE CRICKET SONG

COME CLIMB MY HILL

and

LETTERS FROM CHICKADEE HILL

These words

       These inadequate words

              Are dedicated

      to

      All who seek to find —
      the beauty which sleeps
      in a quiet heart — and
      patiently waits to be
      born again —

Come let us walk among the distant stars
There are no gates — no fences — and no bars.
Out there among the stars we will be free
There are no shadows for the heart to see.

THERE are times — so many many times it seems — when you and I need to walk among the stars — to free the soul from its confinement — to strengthen and renew the spirit — to comfort the troubled heart —

How strangely beautiful it is out there among the stars — where the silence is deep and penetrating — where one can hear one's own heartbeat and know that it belongs to infinity — there are no sounds to our footsteps — only the singing of endless galaxies of stars — there are no shadows — only the twinkling of millions of lights against the curtain of the night — there are no fences to keep one out or to keep one in — there are no barriers to discourage or restrain — out there among the distant stars we shall be as free as the gentle breeze that moves unseen in the darkness —

How strange that there should be no weari-
ness and no fatigue — no anxiety and no worry
— no fear and no hatred — just an acceptance
of all that is beautiful and enduring and true —

I do not need to tell you why we should
walk among the stars — this you will surely
understand — for we are kindred spirits — and
that is why I said to you —

COME

WALK

AMONG

THE

STARS—

The smallest buttercup of molten gold
Has more of beauty than the heart can hold —

For years I never knew — whether the twilight was the ending of the day or the beginning of the night — and then — suddenly one day I understood — that this did not matter at all — for time is but a circle — and so there can be no beginning and no ending — and this is how I came to know that birth and death are one — and it is neither the coming or the going that is of consequence — what is of consequence is the beauty that one gathers in this interlude called life —

And so I have slowly come to understand — that beauty has a thousand different faces — stark branches against a wintry sky — a snowdrop welcoming the spring — the delicate tracery of a spider web — the rich fragrance of the damp woods — the timpani of distant thunder — and yes — do not forget the dusty

pink and molten golds of the sunset — the
music of raindrops upon the leaves — the sleepy
call of a robin in the gathering dusk — and the
glittering stars that fill the darkness with the
symbols of time and space unending —

Beauty holds a thousand different faces
toward the searching heart —

Each raindrop holds within its entity
An image of the vast and ageless sea —

It has been said — by an ancient prophet — that life should be a crystal vase to hold the flowers of happiness — and to reflect the glory of the sun — how beautiful these words and yet how sad — for most of us hold but the broken fragments in our careless hands — perhaps it is but wisdom that our lives are fashioned of many different fragments — for could happiness be complete if we had never walked with sorrow — is not the brightness of hope made more radiant by the darkness of despair — does not pain temper the heart to seek new beauty —

One slowly learns that each fragment — each broken piece — can still reflect the glory of the sun if held toward the light — one comes to understand that each violet holds eternity in its upturned face — each raindrop is no stranger to the sea — each bit of color belongs as does each shadow — to the canvas that each one of us must paint —

There comes a time — when we become aware that each fragment can be fitted to another until the crystal vase will once more hold its flowers —

Do I need to say that an understanding faith can mend any broken vase — any broken thing — even any broken heart —

The crimson fires of sunset burned away
And left the scattered embers of the day —

So MANY years ago — clouds were dreams and fantasies — to one who had never seen the sea — they were ships with strange cargoes — tossed angrily about on the dark and stormy December waves — or drifting idly across the placid blue waters of June — even today one has need to dream a bit — and this is good — one also has to lift the eyes upward to look into the sky — and this too is good —

Clouds add motion to the heavens — sometimes they hide the sun but the sun is still there — sometimes they blot out the stars but the stars do not mind — sometimes they frame the sunsets with changing colors — and remember — that never in eternity will there be two sunsets exactly the same — and so I am grateful that we did not miss the one we shared this

evening — it had a haunting loveliness that
lingered — perhaps because we were so reluc-
tant to have it fade away —

I know that I do not have to tell you what
I am about to write — and yet — I want so very
much that you should remember — that one
sunset shared has more of beauty than a thousand seen alone —

I want so very much for you to remember
this — so very much —

May God be gracious to each lonely one
Who walks in silence toward the setting sun —

WITHIN each heart there is some portion of loneliness — some sense of longing — some need yet unfulfilled — perhaps this is the thread by which one clings to the eternal — a fragile gossamer thread — that stretches across life's seasons as a spider web stretches across the grasses — and catches the dew of morning —

If you have watched the constant stars burn slowly through the lingering folds of darkness — and felt the heaviness of time unmoving — you have come to know its quiet desperation — and surely you must also know — that somewhere in that same darkness there is an answer to the need — for loneliness will vanish when love is near — as darkness fades before the first faint shafts of dawn —

I have learned — as you have learned — that loneliness does not only touch the hearts of

those who are alone — it often comes as slow
and gnawing pain amid one's busy crowded
hours — as wisps of fog move stealthily across
the meadow after a summer shower — for loneliness often springs unbidden from some deep
and quiet place within the heart — and yet we
know — both you and I — that nothing is lost
when loneliness is gone —

If loneliness is the thread which binds us to
the eternal — then love which finds its own
must be eternity unquestioned —

Faith is the promise of the spring's rebirth
When snow is deep upon the waiting earth —

FAITH is the single star that shines in constancy against the dark — it is a thing of the timeless spirit — fragile at birth — fragile as a single strand of cobweb — and yet with strength sufficient to defy the winds of doubt and fear —

Faith often stands alone between the transient and the eternal — as one last leaf clings tenaciously to the branch — refusing to submit to death until the promise of new life is fulfilled — it is a thing of the spirit that can neither be heard nor seen nor felt — but somehow I know that this really is not true — for I have heard faith in the song of the thrush — and seen it in the buds of the spring anemones — and felt it in the soft caress of the wind upon my face —

It is given to all at birth — to be nourished in life as a flower is nourished by the sun and also by the rain — to each of us it shows a different face — for each it must fill its own peculiar need — each must add something of strength from his own soul — and yet I know — that wedded to the faith of one who loves you it becomes a source of understanding and infinite strength — it will bind souls together into the timeless tomorrow — for it was born of the timeless spirit — in the timeless past —

The shadows lengthen as the sun descends
And twilight deepens as the daylight ends —

THERE are no shadows on the world at noon — there are no shadows on the heart when love is near — and yet — and yet as daylight fades toward the dusk — the shadows often lengthen — and sometimes sadness comes stealing up from the place of remembering — for sadness is but a shadow — a shadow that is fashioned from love's bright sunlight shining upon a treasured memory —

How varied are the shadows that rest against the earth — soft and hazy in the summer's warmth — gray and sharply defined upon the autumn hillside — stark and coldly blue against the winter's snow — gentle and ever so softly blurred with the eternal promise of spring's returning —

And sadness too is varied as it lies against the heart — tinged with a wistfulness for one who is missed — acute with anguish where the need is deep and constant — bearable in the brightness of the sunshine — crushing the spirit in the lonely hours before the dawn —

And in remembering that there could be no shadows if there had not been light — I ask myself —

> *Could spring's fresh beauty lift*
> *your heart as high*
> *Had not dark branches etched*
> *the winter sky —*

The stars are daisies in the field of night
Come — help me gather them before the light —

MANY times I have stood alone beneath the stars — and watched them become blurred and indistinct — no — it is not wise to stand alone beneath the stars — for stars are creations of ageless beauty — and beauty that is ageless must be shared lest it be tinged with sorrow — perhaps you know how thin the line that separates beauty from pain — I know this too — for life was created to be shared — and that is why love was brought into this world —

And how did love come into the world you ask — but even now you know the answer — love came into the world with a mother's agony — and that is why love is born of pain — and pain is born of love —

And now you will understand even as I — that love that is not shared will turn into anguish — anguish that sweeps across the soul — as

great clouds sweep across the sky — and hide
the stars from view upon a stormy night —

But tonight the stars are promises — and
promises too need to be shared — to be given
and received — tonight the stars are flowers that
blossom amid the doubts and fears of life — tonight the stars are flowers — and flowers too
must be shared lest they wither and die — and
nothing that is beautiful should ever die — can
ever die —

No life moves shadowless across the land
Each one must leave its footprints in the sand —

My GIFT of life is a thing of transient beauty — a thing of mystery — and above all else a miracle — it is a thing of beauty because of the soul — a mystery because it stretches between the invisible yesterday and the unknown tomorrow — a miracle because it is a composite of countless other lives —

And as my life has been gently touched by other lives — it follows that I have touched theirs too — one cannot always know the time of greatest need — perhaps this is as it should be — perhaps it is only for me to light one darkened corner of the path — to place a hand upon your shoulder as a symbol of my kinship and my love — perhaps I came this way — as did you — to fill some special need — but this is not always given to us to know —

Sometimes a single word will lift the spirit — sometimes words are so inadequate — and sometimes it is destined that one must only listen — sometimes a smile will bridge the empty darkness — sometimes just the nearness is the answer —

From many lives I have gathered courage and strength — I have learned humility and gentleness and forgiveness — and for all of these blessings — I am grateful —

And so you must understand that your life is not your own — it has become a part of mine — and so it follows that my life does not belong to me — it is yours —

As surely as the great tides ebb and flow
Our lives were charted countless worlds ago —

I stood upon a cliff above the sea — and saw far out upon the distant dark — a lighted ship moving slowly upon the trackless waters — I knew — that somewhere in the vast blackness of the night — other ships were keeping upon their charted courses — it is inevitable that somewhere — sometime — two of these shall meet — the course of each was charted in a distant port — and still one knows that even though months and years must pass — it is inevitable that somewhere — sometime — upon the timeless sea — two of these shall meet — and this event must be properly inscribed upon the ship's log — for it is of consequence to all who sail the seas —

Therefore it should not seem strange — that somewhere in the vastness of infinity — your life and mine should meet — your life was charted countless years ago — and so was mine — for lives are not bits of flotsam upon the waters — but proud ships sailing toward a destined meeting place — according to the plan and pattern for creation —

You may believe that your life first touched mine upon this printed page — I do not think that this is true — no — I know that this cannot be true — for I met you once before — a thousand misty years ago — do you not remember —

We gather strength from sadness and from pain
Each time we die we learn to live again —

WHERE does one find strength
— usually where one seeks it — for it is every-
where about — it fills the quiet woods — rides
on the wind that sweeps the mountain top —
and is measured in the restless wings above the
open fields and sunny gardens —

Each living thing has access to the strength
it needs — the hawk glides in widening circles
in the sky — the crow moves with labored beat
of wings — the swallow skims above the earth
with graceful turns — the ruby throat hovers
motionless before the cardinal flower — each
is given the strength it needs to fulfill its pur-
pose in creation — none questions the wisdom
of the Creator —

But you and I are not as wise — we spend our
strength in aimless quests — on things inconse-

quential — in needless worrying — and so we must constantly renew our strength —

You and I need to listen to the deep silence of the woods — to breathe deeply of the solitude upon the mountains — to share the energy of throbbing wings — and someday you and I will come to understand — that we too shall find our strength where we shall seek it —

And as the fury of the storm departs
The rainbow comes to calm our troubled hearts —

THERE can be no rainbow until the storm has passed — and remembering this I gain courage to face the turbulence and the stress —

The earth is strangely hushed and quietly waiting — across the threatening sky bright javelins of light are hurled by unseen hands — the deep voice of the thunder rumbles and complains — there is a flash of wings across the open fields as the feathered creatures seek shelter from the gathering storm — branches stir — restlessly at first — and then with increasing tempo — thrusting upward into the darkening sky —

There is another moment of stillness — and then the waiting rains sweep unopposed across the meadow grasses — pressing them downward to the trembling earth — the fury of the storm increases until our world is purged and purified and washed —

And then the storm subsides — and a rainbow appears upon the far horizon — resting lightly upon the misted hills for only a fleeting moment — and is gone — I am grateful that I did not miss this bit of transient loveliness — for one needs more and more of beauty as each storm comes and goes —

These things of beauty you have shared with me
And beauty shared is life's eternity —

How DEEP and mysterious are the wellsprings of the soul — there are so many questions still unanswered — so much of strength still untouched — so many paths of knowledge still untrod — oftentimes it seems that I shall never fully comprehend — or be able to accept with grace — this loneliness of the spirit — that comes with shattering impact from some secret place deep within the heart —

Why do I need so desperately to hear the notes of the wood thrush amid the darkness of December — or see new leaves on branches bare and bleak beneath the winter sky —

Why is the memory of raindrops on a distant hill more valid than the promise of tomorrow — why does that single star have more meaning and more brilliance than a million others scattered upon the velvet gown of night —

Perhaps you have the answer — and if you do I need to know — is it because the things that are intangible have more of substance than things material — tell me if this be true — and then I shall know that nothing which I wish to keep can ever be lost again — for surely memories are intangible — and if they are a part of my today — then today will be a part of your tomorrow — and of mine —

One needs to learn — it is life's common things
That lift the fledgling soul on spreading wings —

THE MYSTERY of life is great and encompassing — and so one needs to intimately know the common things that fill our days with beauty — how else can one hope to learn life's meaning — for we can neither look backward into the past — nor forward into the future — how very wise this is — for most of us are unaware of the loveliness that abounds in the present —

Have you watched a golden butterfly hold gently to a clover blossom — or felt the softness of raindrops upon an upturned face — or heard the mewing of the gulls above the brooding timeless sea — have you held a daisy in your hand — and known that it is a part of the same mystery that keeps the myriads of stars in their appointed places —

Have you breathed of the fragrance of the

returning spring — and the pungent bitterness of dying leaves — and known that they are one —

Do you remember a single blossom that defied the frost — to tell you that tomorrow will be even more beautiful than today — if you remember this and this alone — you have no reason to fear this great mystery that is life — for you hold its secret deep within your heart.